How to Win Over Audiences: Practical [and Easy-to-Apply] Guide for Producing Content on Multiplatforms

Copyright © 2024 Reginaldo Osnildo

All rights reserved.

PRESENTATION

UNDERSTANDING THE CONCEPT OF MULTIPLATFORM

DEFINING YOUR TARGET AUDIENCE

STRATEGIC CONTENT PLANNING

ADAPTABLE STORYTELLING

MAXIMIZING SEO

USING SOCIAL MEDIA TO YOUR ADVANTAGE

VIDEO CONTENT PRODUCTION

PHOTOGRAPHY AND IMPACT IMAGES

PODCASTING AND DIGITAL AUDIO

BLOGGING AND WRITTEN CONTENT

GRAPHIC DESIGN AND VISUAL BRANDING

DATA ANALYSIS AND FEEDBACK

ENGAGEMENT STRATEGIES

ONLINE ADVERTISING AND PROMOTION

INTEGRATED EMAIL MARKETING

PARTNERSHIPS AND COLLABORATIONS

VIRTUAL EVENTS AND WEBINARS

AUGMENTED AND VIRTUAL REALITY

COMMUNITY MANAGEMENT

CONTENT ACCESSIBILITY

SUSTAINABILITY AND SOCIAL RESPONSIBILITY

CRISIS MANAGEMENT

FUTURE TRENDS IN DIGITAL CONTENT

CONTENT MONETIZATION

FINAL CONSIDERATIONS

REGINALDO OSNILDO

PRESENTATION

Welcome to the universe of digital content, where innovation and creativity meet the vast sea of audiences eager for news. In a world where communication barriers are constantly being redrawn by technology, you are faced with an unprecedented opportunity: the ability to reach, engage and influence people on a global scale. This is where this manual becomes your indispensable ally. "**How to Win Over Audiences: Practical [and Easy-to-Apply] Guide for Producing Content on Multiplatforms**" is more than a book; it is a compass for navigators of the vast digital ocean.

You, a content creator, marketer or communicator, are about to embark on a strategic journey designed to maximize your reach and engagement in a fragmented media landscape. Through the pages of this book, I will share with you my updated insights, synthesizing essential knowledge and offering contributions that promise to facilitate your journey in this very competitive universe.

Ready to unlock the secrets of developing and distributing content that resonates with audiences across multiple platforms? This manual is your treasure map. Here, you'll find practical strategies, up-to-date techniques, and innovative tools, all designed to help you excel in digital communication. We'll break down the concepts and offer solutions you can apply immediately, making your message not just heard, but felt and appreciated by those who really matter: your audience.

From understanding the concept of cross-platform to exploring emerging technologies like augmented and virtual reality, this book covers a full spectrum of topics essential for success in the digital age. In each chapter, you will be guided through specific strategies, with practical examples and applicable advice, always focusing on how you can apply this knowledge to achieve your communication goals.

I invite you to start this journey with us, unfolding each chapter as if it were a new stage in your content strategy. And don't worry, each segment of this book has been carefully designed to complete itself, keeping you engaged and eager for the next step. At the end of this journey, you will not only have a comprehensive understanding of how to reach audiences across multiple platforms, but also a set of enhanced skills, ready to put into practice.

Get ready to dive into the next chapter, where we will explore **"UNDERSTANDING THE CONCEPT OF MULTIPLATFORM"**. Here, we'll uncover the nuances of an increasingly complex media landscape and how you can strategically position yourself to make the most of the opportunities it offers. Are you ready to transform the way you create and share content? Let's go on this journey together!

Yours sincerely

Reginaldo Osnildo

UNDERSTANDING THE CONCEPT OF MULTIPLATFORM

In this chapter, you will delve into the heart of contemporary digital communication: the multiplatform landscape. In a world where the boundaries between online and offline are becoming increasingly blurred, understanding how your message can travel harmoniously across different mediums is crucial to success. Let's explore what it means to be cross-platform and why taking an integrated approach is essential to reaching diverse audiences.

THE ERA OF MEDIA FRAGMENTATION

The first thing you need to understand is that we live in an era of media fragmentation. Your potential followers are spread across a wide range of platforms: social media, blogs, podcasts, online videos, and more. Each of these platforms has its own characteristics, language and, most importantly, its own audience. The challenge here is learning to navigate this complex ecosystem, ensuring that your message not only reaches, but also resonates with each segment of your audience.

WHY MULTIPLATFORM?

Adopting a cross-platform approach means more than simply being present in more than one place. It means understanding the nuances of each platform and adapting your message so that it fits perfectly in each context, while maintaining a coherence that strengthens your brand or core message. This is crucial for several reasons:

- **Extended Reach** : Each platform has its own set of unique users. By diversifying your presence, you maximize the total number of people who can be exposed to your content.

- **Deep engagement** : Different types of content resonate in different ways on each platform. Adapting your approach allows you to create deeper connections with your audience.

- **Digital resilience** : Depending on a single platform is risky. The rules of the game can change quickly, impacting your reach and visibility. A multiplatform strategy ensures a more stable and controllable presence.

HOW TO APPROACH STRATEGICALLY

- **Know your platforms** : Start with detailed research into the platforms your target audience spends their time on. Each has its own best practices, preferred content types, and engagement spikes.

- **Core message, multiple expressions** : Develop a strong, clear core message that will be the heart of your content across all platforms. Then adapt it to fit the specifics of each channel.

- **Create complementary content** : Use different platforms to offer different types of value. For example, while videos can be used to entertain and educate, social media can be used for quick updates and direct engagement.

- **Integration and coherence** : Make sure all your platforms are logically interconnected, allowing users to easily navigate between them. Visual and thematic consistency is essential.

Now that you understand the importance of taking a cross-platform approach, it's time to start applying these concepts to your own work. In the next chapter, "**DEFINING YOUR TARGET AUDIENCE**", we will dive into the art of identifying and understanding diverse audiences on specific platforms. This step is essential before planning your content strategy, as knowing who you are trying to reach is the basis of any effective communication.

Ready to deepen your knowledge and adapt your strategy to reach and engage your audience across multiple channels? Let's go on this journey together, discovering how to map your target audience and how this understanding can transform your approach to content. Join us in the next chapter to explore this vital topic.

DEFINING YOUR TARGET AUDIENCE

The journey towards winning over audiences on multiple platforms necessarily involves a deep understanding of who the people on the other side of the screen are. In this chapter, you will learn not only how to identify your target audience, but also understand their needs, wants, and behaviors across different platforms. This is the key to developing content that truly resonates with your audiences and drives meaningful engagement.

WHAT IS TARGET AUDIENCE?

Target audience is a term that describes a specific group of people that you target with your message or content. These people share similar characteristics, such as age, geographic location, interests, challenges, or behaviors. Understanding these characteristics is crucial to shaping your communication effectively.

THE IMPORTANCE OF DEFINED YOUR AUDIENCE

- **Effective Targeting** : By knowing your audience, you can create content that speaks directly to their interests and needs.

- **Resource optimization** : Focusing on a specific audience allows you to optimize your time and resources, directing efforts where they will really make a difference.

– **Increased engagement** : Relevant and personalized content is more likely to generate engagement as it resonates more deeply with the audience.

- **Improved results** : Targeted communication leads to more tangible results, whether sales, registrations, participation or any other success metric.

METHODS FOR IDENTIFYING YOUR TARGET AUDIENCE

- **Demographic analysis** : Start by defining the basic characteristics of your audience, such as age, gender, location and education level. Tools like Google Analytics and social media insights can provide this information.

- Surveys and Quizzes : Use online quizzes to collect information directly from your audience. Open-ended questions can reveal insights into your preferences and behaviors.

- Study of online behavior : Observing how your audience interacts with different types of content on platforms can reveal a lot about their likes and dislikes.

- Psychographic segmentation : In addition to demographic characteristics, understanding your audience's personality, values, attitudes, interests and lifestyle is key to creating messages that resonate on a more personal level.

APPLYING YOUR AUDIENCE'S KNOWLEDGE

Once you have a clear understanding of who your target audience is, it's time to apply that knowledge to develop an effective content strategy. This includes choosing the right platforms to reach them, the type of content that generates the most value for them, and the language that best speaks to their heart and mind.

Now that you know who your audience is and what they want, the next step is to plan how to meet these expectations in a strategic and coherent way across all platforms where they are present. In the next chapter, "**STRATEGIC CONTENT PLANNING**," we'll explore how to develop a coherent content plan that not only meets, but exceeds your target audience's expectations, keeping your brand relevant and your message resonant amid the constantly evolving landscape. digital.

Get ready to dive into the nuances of content planning, a crucial step that serves as the backbone of any successful communications strategy. Together, we'll discover how to turn your understanding of your target audience into a winning content strategy that leverages your success across multiple platforms. Continue with us on this engaging and transformative

REGINALDOOSNILDO

journey.

STRATEGIC CONTENT PLANNING

After precisely defining your target audience, the next step is to draw up a strategic content plan that effectively reaches them across multiple platforms. This chapter is dedicated to helping you develop a coherent, comprehensive content plan capable of engaging your audience in any medium. The key to success is the consistency, relevance and adaptability of your content.

THE FOUNDATION OF STRATEGIC CONTENT PLANNING

Strategic content planning starts with a clear understanding of your goals. Do you want to increase brand awareness? Generate leads? Establish authority in your niche? Setting clear, measurable goals is the first step to creating a plan that meets your needs and those of your audience.

GETTING TO KNOW THE PLATFORMS

Each platform has its own set of rules, audience and types of content that perform best. Part of strategic planning is understanding these differences and using this knowledge to your advantage. It's not enough to replicate the same content across all channels; it is necessary to adapt it to meet the specific expectations of each platform, maintaining a coherent narrative.

STEPS TO EFFICIENT CONTENT PLANNING

- **Content audit** : Review existing content to understand what works, what doesn't, and identify gaps.

- **Definition of themes and formats** : Based on the interests of your target audience and the particularities of each platform, define central themes and the most appropriate content formats.

- **Editorial calendar** : Create a detailed content calendar, planning what will be published, when and where. This helps you maintain consistency and take advantage of important dates or seasonal events.

- **Content production and adaptation** : Develop content that not only informs and entertains, but is also aligned with your goals. Remember to adapt the tone and format of the content for each platform.

- Distribution and promotion : Plan how you will distribute and promote your content. Include organic and paid strategies to expand your reach.

- Measure and adjust : Set relevant success metrics and track your content performance regularly. Be ready to adjust your strategy as needed.

MAINTAINING COHERENCE

Across all platforms, maintain consistency with your brand and message. Your audience should recognize your voice and values no matter where they interact with your content. This consistency helps build trust and strengthen your online presence.

With a strategic content plan in hand, the next challenge is to adapt your narrative to different formats and platforms without losing its essence. In the next chapter, "**ADAPTABLE STORYTELLING**," we'll explore techniques for telling your story effectively, regardless of the medium. We'll learn how to adjust tone, style, and approach to capture your audience's attention and keep them engaged, no matter where they are.

Be ready to dive into the art of adaptive storytelling, a crucial component for any content creator who wants to maximize the impact of their message in a diverse digital landscape. Continue with us on this strategic journey to discover how to make your stories not just heard, but lived and remembered by your audience.

ADAPTABLE STORYTELLING

In the art of winning audiences in a fragmented media ecosystem, the ability to tell stories that captivate and retain audience attention, regardless of platform, is more valuable than ever. This chapter is dedicated to exploring the concept of adaptive storytelling — the art of shaping your narratives to fit seamlessly into the various communication channels available, while keeping their essence intact.

THE HEART OF ADAPTABLE STORYTELLING

At the heart of adaptive storytelling is the understanding that each platform has its own language, preferences, and expectations. A well-told Instagram story, with its emphasis on impactful visuals and short text, needs a different approach when transposed to a podcast, for example, where auditory storytelling and detailed development prevail.

STRATEGIES TO ADAPT YOUR NARRATIVE

- **Know the platform** : Start with a deep understanding of the characteristics of each platform. This includes the type of content that performs best, typical audience behavior, and the tools available to content creators.

- **Core Message** : Identify the heart of your story — the central message you want to convey. This message must remain consistent regardless of what form the story takes on different platforms.

- **Adapt the packaging** : Adjust the "packaging" of your story — format, style, tone — to suit the medium. This could mean turning an in-depth blog post into a series of Twitter posts, a long-form video into an impactful snippet for Instagram, or a visual story into an engaging episode for a podcast.

- **Interactive engagement** : Use the unique characteristics of each platform to make the story more interactive. Polls on Instagram, threads on Twitter, and live Q&As on YouTube are examples of how you can engage your audience and get them to actively participate in the narrative.

- **Visual and thematic consistency** : Maintain visual and thematic consistency across all platforms. This helps strengthen your brand and makes it easier for your audience to recognize, regardless of where they consume your content.

PRACTICAL EXAMPLE

Imagine you want to tell the story of how your sustainable coffee company impacts local communities. On Instagram, you share impactful images of coffee plantations and short videos of farmers, with captions that summarize their positive impacts. On your blog, you publish a detailed article about the sustainable production process. On YouTube, a short documentary showing the daily lives of communities. And finally, on LinkedIn, an opinion article about the importance of sustainability in the coffee sector. Each piece of content offers a unique take on the story, tailored to the medium in which it is shared.

With adaptive storytelling strategies in hand, the next step is to ensure that your content is found by your audience. In the next chapter, "**MAXIMIZING SEO**," we'll dive into techniques and strategies for optimizing your content for search engines, ensuring your message not only reaches but also engages the right audience on the right platforms.

Be ready to explore the world of SEO and learn how small tweaks can mean big improvements in your content's visibility. Together, we will ensure that your stories are not only told, but heard and seen by as many people as possible. Continue this journey with us and transform your content into an unstoppable force in the digital universe.

MAXIMIZING SEO

Now that you know how to adapt your stories for different platforms, ensuring they resonate with your audience, the next step is to ensure those stories are found. In this chapter, we will explore how to maximize the visibility of your content through SEO (Search Engine Optimization) techniques, focusing especially on web content. SEO is your bridge to connecting with those who are actively searching for the information, solutions or inspiration you can offer.

UNDERSTANDING SEO

SEO is the set of practices designed to improve the position of a website or page on the results page of search engines such as Google. This is crucial as most online experiences start with a search. Being well positioned in search results means more visibility, more visits to your website and, consequently, greater potential for engagement and conversion.

KEY STRATEGIES TO MAXIMIZE SEO

- **Keyword research** : Start by identifying the keywords your target audience uses to search for content related to yours. Tools like Google Keyword Planner or SEMrush can help. Incorporate these keywords naturally in your titles, subtitles and throughout the content.

- **On-page optimization** : In addition to keywords, ensure that every page on your website is optimized for search engines. This includes meta titles and descriptions, user-friendly URLs, and the use of header tags (H1, H2, etc.) to clearly structure your content.

- **Quality and relevant content** : Search engines prioritize content that is useful and informative for users. Make sure your content is original, valuable, and well-crafted, addressing your audience's needs and questions.

- **User experience** : Ease of navigation on the website, page loading speed and responsiveness for mobile devices are factors that influence ranking in search engines. A good user experience is fundamental.

- **Link building** : Building a network of internal links and obtaining external links from trusted sites can increase your site's authority in search engines. This includes using internal links to connect different content on your website and look for quality backlink opportunities.

- **SEO for videos and images** : Don't forget to optimize multimedia content. This includes using relevant titles, descriptions, and tags for your videos and ensuring images have descriptive file names and alt text to improve accessibility and indexing.

PUTTING IT INTO PRACTICE

Implementing an effective SEO strategy takes time and dedication, but the long-term benefits are invaluable. Start with small tweaks and keep testing and learning to understand what works best for your content and audience.

With your content now optimized for search engines, the next step is to ensure it shines on social media. In the next chapter, "**USING SOCIAL MEDIA TO YOUR ADVANTAGE**", we will explore strategies to optimize your presence on social media platforms and further engage your audience. Social media is a vital complement to SEO, providing another powerful avenue to reach and engage with your audience.

Get ready to dive into social media best practices, learning how each platform can serve your unique content goals and how you can leverage these channels to expand your reach and strengthen your brand. Continue on this journey with us and discover how to transform social networks into powerful allies in spreading your message.

USING SOCIAL MEDIA TO YOUR ADVANTAGE

As we navigate the digital age, social media has become fertile ground for cultivating connections, engaging audiences and expanding the reach of your content. In this chapter, we'll explore how you can optimize your presence on social media, turning it into powerful communication vehicles for your brand or message.

THE ART OF ENGAGING ON SOCIAL MEDIA

Engaging audiences on social media goes beyond simply posting content. It involves creating genuine connections, fostering communities and consistently providing value. Here are some strategies to elevate your social media presence:

- **Know your audience** : Use demographic and engagement data available in social media analysis tools to understand who your audience is, what they value and how they prefer to interact.

- **Adapted and authentic content** : Each platform has its own set of standards and expectations. Adapt your content to each of them, maintaining its authenticity. What works on Instagram may not work on LinkedIn, and vice versa.

- **Interactivity and dialogue** : Encourage interaction through questions, polls and calls to action. Respond to comments and messages in a timely manner to foster a sense of community.

- **Consistency and frequency** : Establish a consistent posting schedule, but avoid sacrificing quality for quantity. Consistency helps build expectation in your audience, while quality ensures they remain engaged.

- **Use attractive visuals** : Social media is highly visual. Use high-quality images, videos, and graphics to capture attention and convey your message effectively.

- **Stories and real moments** : Stories features on platforms like Instagram and Facebook offer a great opportunity to share everyday moments, behind-the-scenes and limited-time content that can increase intimacy with your audience.

- **Monitoring and analysis** : Use analysis tools to monitor the performance of your content, adjusting your strategies as necessary. Understanding what resonates with your audience allows you to continually improve your approach.

TAKING ADVANTAGE OF SPECIFIC PLATFORMS

- **Instagram** : Excellent for visual content and storytelling through images, short videos and stories. Ideal for brands with a strong aesthetic component or visual products.

- **Facebook** : Great for communities, sharing events and content that encourages engagement and discussions.

- **Twitter** : Ideal for quick updates, dialogue with the audience and participation in current trends and conversations.

– **LinkedIn** : Best for professional content, thought leadership articles, and networking.

CHALLENGES AND OPPORTUNITIES

Social networks are dynamic environments, subject to constant changes in algorithms and trends. Staying up to date with these changes and adapting your strategy accordingly is crucial to keeping your content relevant and engaging.

Equipped with strategies to maximize your social media presence, the next chapter will guide you through the world of "**VIDEO CONTENT PRODUCTION**". Videos are one of the most effective ways to capture audience attention on social media and beyond. Let's explore how to create compelling videos that can be shared across multiple platforms, increasing your reach and engagement.

Get ready to unlock the potential of videos in your content strategy by learning best practices and tips for producing visual content that not only informs and entertains, but also inspires and connects. Join us on this journey to transform your ideas into impactful videos that capture the essence of your message and expand your digital reach.

VIDEO CONTENT PRODUCTION

As we progress on this digital journey, it becomes increasingly clear that video content is one of the most powerful tools for capturing attention and engaging audiences. Whether on social media, websites or streaming platforms, videos offer a dynamic and immersive way to tell stories. In this chapter, we'll explore how to create compelling videos that can be shared across multiple platforms, expanding your reach and reinforcing your message.

WHY VIDEOS?

Videos have the power to convey emotions, share complex information in an understandable way, and create deep connections with the viewer. They are also highly shareable, which makes them perfect for increasing the reach of your content. With the growing consumption of online video, ignoring this format could mean missing a valuable opportunity to engage your audience.

PLANNING AND STRATEGY

Before starting to produce video content, it is important to clearly define your objectives. Ask yourself: what do you want to achieve with your videos? Increase brand awareness? Educate your audience? Generate sales? The answer will guide content strategy, helping to define the themes, tone and style of your videos. Once the objectives are clear, follow these steps for effective planning:

- **Define your target audience** : Understanding who your audience is is crucial to determining the style of video that will resonate most with them. This influences everything from the language used to the topics covered.

- **Choose the type of video** : There are several video formats you can explore — tutorials, testimonials, behind-the-scenes stories, webinars, and more. The choice depends on your objective and what most engages your audience.

- **Scripting and storyboarding** : Planning your content

through scripts and storyboards can help organize your ideas and ensure that the message is delivered clearly and efficiently.

- **Equipment and production** : You don't need the most expensive equipment to create quality videos. Many current smartphones have cameras capable of filming in high definition. However, investing in a good microphone can significantly improve the quality of your video.

- **Editing** : Editing is where the magic happens. Use editing software to cut, add transitions, effects, text and music, transforming raw recordings into engaging and professional content.

- **Optimization for different platforms** : Make sure your videos are optimized for each platform. This may mean adjusting formats, durations and even calls to action, according to the specifics of each channel.

TIPS FOR ENGAGING VIDEOS

- **Keep it short and to the point** : The online audience's attention span is limited. Short, to-the-point videos tend to work best, especially on social media.

- **Invest in audio quality** : A video with bad audio can turn off viewers. Investing in a good microphone is essential to maintain quality.

- **Include subtitles** : Many people watch videos in public, with the sound turned off. Captions not only make your content accessible to everyone, they also increase the chances of message retention.

- **Make good use of the first second** : Capture the viewer's attention from the beginning. Use the first few seconds to spark curiosity or introduce the value your video will offer.

Now that you're equipped with best practices for creating video content, it's time to explore another crucial visual element in digital communication: photography. In the next chapter, "**PHOTOGRAPHY AND IMPACT IMAGES**", we'll discover how powerful images can complement your video and text content, helping to capture your audience's attention and convey your message effectively.

Get ready to dive into the world of photography, where a picture can be worth a thousand words, opening new doors for engagement and expanding your digital reach. Continue with us on this engaging and transformative journey, where each chapter brings you even closer to success in the digital universe.

PHOTOGRAPHY AND IMPACT IMAGES

In an increasingly visual world, photography and images have become indispensable tools in the art of telling stories and engaging audiences. This chapter explores how you can use impactful images to complement your content, capture your audience's attention, and convey powerful messages without the need for many words.

THE POWER OF THE IMAGE

An impactful image can evoke emotions, tell an entire story, or highlight a key point with a single glance. On digital platforms, where competition for user attention is intense, images not only help break the monotony of text, but also significantly increase engagement and information retention.

SELECTING THE RIGHT IMAGE

- **Relevance** : The image must be aligned with the content. It needs to reinforce the message you want to convey, not distract or confuse it.

- **-Quality** : Choose high quality images. Pixelated or low-resolution images can detract from the perceived professionalism of your brand or content.

Originality : Whenever possible, use original images. Unique photographs can help your content stand out in a sea of repetition.

- **Emotion** : Images that evoke emotion tend to have a greater impact. Think about the feeling you want to evoke in your audience and select images that reflect that.

TIPS FOR CREATING IMPACT IMAGES

- **Composition** : Learn the basic principles of photographic composition, such as the rule of thirds, to create balanced and attractive images.

- **Lighting** : Lighting can completely transform a photo.

Try to capture images in good natural light or learn basic lighting techniques to improve your photos.

- Editing : Use editing tools to adjust contrast, brightness, saturation and other elements that can improve the quality of your image. However, avoid exaggerations that could distort the message.

- Caption and context : When using images in conjunction with text, make sure that the caption or context provided complements and expands the understanding of the image.

IMAGES AND LEGISLATION

When using images, it is essential to respect copyright. Choose your own images, purchase licenses from image banks or use public domain resources and under Creative Commons licenses, always giving credit when necessary.

With the power of images on your side, the next chapter takes you into the world of "**PODCASTING AND DIGITAL AUDIO**". We'll explore how audio content can complement your digital communications arsenal, allowing you to reach your audience in new and profound ways, even when they can't be looking at a screen.

Get ready to unlock the potential of podcasts and audio content by learning how to plan, produce and promote episodes that can educate, entertain and inspire your audience. Continue with us on this journey, where each chapter opens new horizons in your digital content strategy.

PODCASTING AND DIGITAL AUDIO

As the digital world evolves, podcasting and digital audio content are emerging as powerful communication vehicles. Allowing you to reach your audience in unique and personal ways, podcasts have the advantage of being consumed while your audience carries out other activities, such as driving, walking or doing household chores. In this chapter, we'll explore how you can integrate podcasting and digital audio into your content strategy to deeply engage with your audience.

WHY INVEST IN PODCASTING?

- **Accessibility** : Podcasts are accessible and easy to consume. Your audience can listen to them anywhere, anytime, using just a smartphone and headphones.

- **Personal connection** : The audio format allows for an intimate and personal connection with the audience, creating a sense of direct dialogue between you and your listeners.

- **Niche markets** : Podcasting offers the opportunity to explore specific market niches with highly targeted content, building a community of loyal listeners.

FIRST STEPS TO CREATING YOUR PODCAST

- **Define your theme and audience** : Choose a theme that you are passionate about and that resonates with your target audience. Having a clear focus will help attract and retain listeners interested in the topic.

- **Choose the format** : Interviews, monologues, panel discussions, or a mix of formats — decide what best suits your content and style.

- **Invest in quality equipment** : Audio quality is crucial in podcasts. A good microphone and decent acoustics can make all the difference.

- **Plan and produce your episodes** : Outline key talking points and do adequate research to ensure informative and engaging content. Regularity in publishing episodes is also important to keep the audience engaged.

- **Editing** : Editing can significantly improve the quality of your podcast by removing errors, unnecessary pauses, and adding music or sound effects to enrich the listening experience.

- **Distribution** : Platforms like Spotify, Apple Podcasts and Google Podcasts are essential for reaching a wider audience. Use podcast aggregators to distribute your content efficiently.

- **Promotion** : Use your social networks, website and any other communication channel to promote your podcast. Considering transcribing episodes into blog articles or social media content can also help attract a larger audience.

ENGAGING YOUR AUDIENCE

- **Ask for feedback** : Encourage your listeners to leave comments and suggestions. This not only provides valuable information to improve your content, but also increases engagement with your audience.

- **Create a community** : Use social media or online forums to create a community around your podcast, where listeners can discuss episodes and share ideas.

Armed with the strategies for creating an engaging and informative podcast, you're ready to explore other forms of digital content. In the next chapter, "**BLOGGING AND WRITTEN CONTENT**," we'll return to the roots of online communication to discover how articles, blog posts, and other written formats continue to be critical for engaging audiences and strengthening your digital presence.

Be ready to deepen your storytelling skills and share information impactfully through text, complementing your video and audio strategies for a truly multidimensional online presence. Stick with us as we explore the art and science behind effective written content.

BLOGGING AND WRITTEN CONTENT

As the digital world advances rapidly, with new forms of content constantly emerging, blogging and written content maintain their place as fundamental pillars of online communication. This chapter will dive into the art and science behind effective blogging and written content creation, showing how they can complement your video and audio strategies for a comprehensive and impactful online presence.

THE IMPORTANCE OF WRITTEN CONTENT

- **SEO** : Written content is crucial for search engine optimization. Well-written articles, with strategic use of keywords, can significantly increase your website's visibility.

- **Authority** : Publishing informative, well-researched content establishes you or your brand as an authority in your field, building trust with your audience.

– **Shareable** : Written content is easily shareable, which can help broaden your reach and attract new audiences.

HOW TO CREATE ENGAGING WRITTEN CONTENT

- **Know your audience** : Understanding who your audience is and what they are looking for is the first step to creating content that resonates and engages.

- **Attractive titles** : A good title is essential to attract attention. It should be intriguing and clear, indicating the value the reader will gain from dedicating their time to your content.

- **Clear structure** : Use subheadings, lists, and short paragraphs to make your content easy to scan. Many readers prefer to preview content before committing to reading in detail.

- **Valuable content** : Provide useful information, unique insights, or solutions to common problems. Real value keeps readers coming back.

- **Calls to action (CTAs)** : Include clear calls to action, encouraging readers to engage more with your content, whether by commenting, sharing or following links to learn more.

- **SEO Optimization** : In addition to including relevant keywords, make sure your content is optimized for SEO in other aspects, such as meta descriptions and friendly URLs.

- **Regularity** : Maintaining a consistent publishing schedule helps you build a loyal audience and improves your search engine rankings.

MEASURING SUCCESS

Use analytical tools to track the performance of your content. Metrics like page views, average time on page, and bounce rates can offer valuable insights into what works and what needs to be tweaked.

INTEGRATING WITH OTHER FORMS OF CONTENT

Written content should not exist in isolation. Integrate it with your video, audio and image content for a rich and varied user experience. For example, summarize key points from a podcast in a blog article or supplement a post with infographics.

Equipped with the techniques to create engaging and effective written content, the next step is to explore how graphic design and visual branding play a crucial role in digital communication. In the next chapter, **"GRAPHIC DESIGN AND VISUAL BRANDING"**, we will uncover how to use visual elements to strengthen your message and create a consistent and memorable brand identity.

Get ready to discover how visual aesthetics can amplify the impact of your content and captivate your audience even more deeply. Continue with us on this journey of exploring integral digital communication, where each element works together to build a truly impactful online presence.

GRAPHIC DESIGN AND VISUAL BRANDING

In this chapter, we will explore the vast world of graphic design and visual branding, crucial elements for any successful digital communications strategy. A strong, cohesive brand identity, supported by quality graphic design, not only captures your audience's attention but also conveys your brand's message clearly and memorably.

THE IMPORTANCE OF GRAPHIC DESIGN AND VISUAL BRANDING

- **First impression** : Visuals are often the first point of contact between your brand and the public. An impactful design can make the difference between catching attention or being ignored.

- **Effective communication** : In addition to attracting attention, graphic design helps communicate your message more effectively, making it easier to understand and retain information.

- **Brand consistency** : A consistent visual identity across platforms and content types helps build brand awareness and loyalty.

FUNDAMENTAL ELEMENTS OF GRAPHIC DESIGN AND VISUAL BRANDING

- **Logo and visual identity** : Your logo and associated visual elements (color palette, typography, etc.) must reflect the personality and values of your brand. They must be easily recognizable and versatile enough to work across different media and contexts.

- **Images and graphics** : Use high-quality images and graphics that complement and reinforce your message. Consider using original or custom images to stand out.

- **Layouts and templates** : Develop consistent layouts and templates for your website, blog posts, newsletters and any other communication material. This not only saves time but also reinforces visual cohesion.

- **Adaptability for platforms** : Make sure your design is adaptable for different platforms, maintaining integrity and effectiveness across mobile, desktop and print devices.

TIPS FOR CREATING EFFECTIVE VISUAL BRANDING

- **Simplicity** : Less is often more in design. A simple and clear approach can be much more effective for communication and memorization.

- **Brand story** : Integrate elements of your brand's storytelling into the design. This might include choosing colors that represent your mission or images that reflect your values.

- **Feedback and testing** : Get feedback from your audience and do A/B testing when possible to understand what works best in terms of design and branding.

- **Professionalism** : If possible, invest in graphic design professionals. An amateur design can give your brand a negative image.

MEASURING IMPACT

As with other areas of digital marketing, it's important to measure the impact of your visual design and branding. Analytics tools can help you understand how visual elements are influencing engagement, brand awareness, and conversions.

INTEGRATING DESIGN AND CONTENT

Remember, graphic design and visual branding should not exist in isolation from the rest of your content. They must work together with text, video, audio, and any other type of content to create a cohesive and engaging user experience.

With a solid understanding of how graphic design and visual branding can strengthen your digital communications strategy, we're ready to move into data analysis and feedback. In the next chapter, **"DATA ANALYSIS AND FEEDBACK,"** we'll explore how to use analytics and user feedback to evaluate the performance of your content and adjust your strategies to maximize success.

Be ready to dive into the world of data, where every interaction and engagement can provide valuable insights to optimize your digital presence. Stay with us as we move forward to make your digital communications more effective and data-driven.

DATA ANALYSIS AND FEEDBACK

In the world of digital marketing and communications, data analysis and user feedback are essential to understand the performance of your content and the effectiveness of your strategies. This chapter will guide you through the process of collecting, interpreting, and applying data and feedback to optimize your digital content initiatives.

THE IMPORTANCE OF DATA ANALYSIS

- **Understand user behavior** : Analytics data offers insights into how users interact with your content, enabling adjustments focused on increasing engagement and retention.

- **Measure success** : Defining and monitoring key metrics helps you assess whether your communication goals are being met, guiding future decisions.

- **Identify trends and patterns** : Data analysis can reveal content consumption trends and user behavior patterns, providing a foundation for proactive strategies.

ESSENTIAL TOOLS AND METRICS

- **Google Analytics** : Essential for analyzing website traffic, navigation patterns, traffic sources and conversions.

- **Social media tools** : Platforms like Facebook Insights and Twitter Analytics offer data on content performance, reach, engagement and audience demographics.

- **Key metrics** : Engagement (likes, shares, comments), reach, website traffic, time on page, bounce rates, and conversions are some of the most important metrics to track.

COLLECTING AND USING FEEDBACK

- **Surveys and quizzes** : Tools like Google Forms or SurveyMonkey can help collect direct feedback from your audience about the quality and relevance of your content.

- **Comments on social media and blogs** : Monitor and respond to comments to understand audience reactions and perceptions towards your content.

- **A/B testing** : Use A/B testing to try different approaches to your content and design, measuring which version performs best with your audience.

APPLYING DATA AND FEEDBACK

- **Adjusting strategies** : Use the data collected to refine your content strategies, focusing on formats, topics and channels that generate better engagement.

- **Content personalization** : User behavior insights can help personalize content for different audience segments, increasing relevance and impact.

- **Innovation and experimentation** : Encourage innovation by experimenting with new formats and approaches, using data and feedback as guides for these explorations.

With a solid understanding of how to analyze data and integrate feedback to improve your content strategies, you are well positioned to explore the nuances of "**ENGAGEMENT STRATEGIES**". In the next chapter, we'll dive into specific techniques for fostering audience interaction with your content, turning passive views into active engagements and building a vibrant community around your brand or message.

Get ready to learn the art of deeply engaging with your audience, encouraging active participation and dialogue, key elements for lasting success in today's dynamic digital landscape. Stay with us as we move forward on this enriching journey, each step bringing us closer to more impactful and meaningful digital communication.

ENGAGEMENT STRATEGIES

Engaging your audience isn't just about generating views or clicks; it's about creating a meaningful connection that encourages active participation and builds a community around your brand or message. In this chapter, we'll explore effective strategies for increasing audience engagement, turning passive followers into active participants and advocates for your brand.

UNDERSTANDING ENGAGEMENT

Engagement goes beyond numbers. It's about the quality of the interactions you have with your audience. Comments, shares, likes and viewing time are indicative of how relevant and impactful your content is to the audience. A successful engagement strategy turns your audience into an active community, increasing brand loyalty and the organic reach of your content.

STRATEGIES TO FOSTER ENGAGEMENT

- **Interactive content** : Use formats that invite interaction, such as polls, quizzes, and clear calls to action. Social networks offer specific tools for this, take advantage of them.

- **Value the community** : Respond to comments, messages and emails. Showing that you are listening and valuing audience feedback and contributions encourages more interactions.

- **Quality content** : Keep the content relevant, useful and interesting. Content that solves problems, inspires or educates tends to generate more engagement.

- **Consistency** : Maintain a regular frequency of publications. This helps build a habit among your audience of searching for and interacting with your content.

- **Personalization** : Use data to target your content to different parts of your audience. Personalized content generates greater relevance and, in turn, greater engagement.

- **Community and co-creation** : Encourage your audience to contribute content, whether through contests, hashtags or calls for collaboration. This not only increases engagement, but also the feeling of belonging to the brand.

- **Use Storytelling** : Stories that evoke emotions or are relatable increase the emotional connection with the audience, encouraging interaction.

MEASURING AND ANALYZING ENGAGEMENT

Use analytical tools to monitor engagement. This includes metrics like engagement rate, comments, shares, and community growth. Analyzing this data allows you to adjust strategies and continually improve engagement with your audience.

PRACTICAL EXAMPLES

- **Q&A sessions** : Holding live Q&A sessions on social media can significantly increase engagement by creating a space for direct interaction.

- **User generated content (UGC)** : Encouraging users to share their own experiences related to your brand or content can generate organic engagement and authentic content.

With solid engagement strategies in hand, the next step is to learn how to further expand the reach of your content. In the next chapter, "**ONLINE ADVERTISING AND PROMOTION**," we'll explore how to use paid advertising and other promotion techniques to increase the visibility of your content and attract a larger audience.

Be ready to dive into promotion tactics that can complement your organic efforts, helping you achieve specific marketing and communications goals. Advance with us on this journey, equipped to engage and expand your audience across the vast digital landscape.

ONLINE ADVERTISING AND PROMOTION

After establishing a solid foundation of organic engagement, online advertising and promotion techniques can significantly expand the reach of your content, bringing in new audiences and reinforcing your brand's digital presence. In this chapter, we'll cover how to integrate paid advertising into your content strategy, maximizing the visibility and impact of your work.

UNDERSTANDING ONLINE ADVERTISING

Online advertising involves several forms of paid promotion that can help achieve specific goals, such as increasing brand awareness, driving traffic to a website, or converting leads into customers. Platforms like Google Ads, Facebook Ads and Instagram Ads offer robust tools for segmenting audiences, personalizing messages and measuring the success of your campaigns.

PLANNING YOUR CAMPAIGN

- **Define your objectives** : Specify what you want to achieve with the campaign. This can range from increasing visibility for a new product to promoting an event.

- **Identify your target audience** : Use demographics, interests and behaviors to define who you want to reach. Effective targeting is crucial to campaign success.

- **Choose the right platform** : Select the advertising platform that best aligns with your goals and where your audience spends the most time.

- **Budget and schedule** : Define how much you are willing to spend and the campaign period. Most platforms allow you to adjust your budget in real time based on performance.

- **Create compelling content** : Develop visually appealing ads with clear messages that appeal to your target audience. Test different formats to see what generates the most engagement.

BEST PRACTICES FOR PROMOTION

- **Continuous optimization** : Monitor your campaign performance and make adjustments as needed to improve results.

- **A/B testing** : Test different versions of your ads to determine which elements (images, texts, calls to action) are most effective.

- **Retargeting** : Use retargeting to reach people who have already interacted with your brand, personalizing messages to increase the likelihood of conversion.

- **Integrate with organic content** : Ensure your paid campaigns complement and reinforce your organic efforts, creating a cohesive user experience.

MEASURING SUCCESS

Use specific metrics such as impressions, clicks, conversion rate, and return on investment (ROI) to evaluate the success of your campaign. Analyzing this data allows you to refine your strategies and ensure that your advertising investment brings the desired results.

With a strategic approach to online advertising and promotion, you're ready to explore new frontiers in your content strategy. In the next chapter, "**INTEGRATED EMAIL MARKETING**", we will discuss how email marketing can be harmoniously integrated into your cross-platform content strategy, providing a direct and personalized channel to engage your audience.

Be prepared to discover how to use email marketing to nurture leads, build customer loyalty and reinforce your brand's presence. Advance with us, as each chapter enriches your repertoire of strategies for mastering digital communication.

INTEGRATED EMAIL MARKETING

Email marketing remains one of the most effective and direct tools for communicating with your audience. When integrated into your cross-platform content strategy, it offers a unique channel to reach your audience in a personalized way, nurture leads and foster brand loyalty. This chapter explores how you can use email marketing strategically to complement and amplify the impact of your digital content.

WHY INTEGRATE EMAIL MARKETING?

- **Direct reach** : Email allows you to communicate directly with your audience, delivering relevant content directly to your followers' inboxes.

- **Personalization** : With segmentation and automation, it is possible to personalize your messages according to users' preferences and behaviors, increasing the relevance and effectiveness of communication.

- **Measurement of results** : Email marketing platforms offer detailed analyzes on opens, clicks and conversions, allowing precise adjustments and a better understanding of your audience.

STRATEGIES FOR EFFECTIVE EMAIL MARKETING

- **Build your email list** : Offer value in exchange for the email address, such as e-books, webinars, discounts, to encourage voluntary signups and build an engaged list.

- **Audience segmentation** : Divide your email list into segments based on interest, purchasing behavior or stage in the sales funnel to send more relevant and personalized content.

- **Valuable content** : In addition to promotions, include useful and informative content that educates and entertains your audience, reinforcing the perception of your brand's value.

- **Attractive design** : Use responsive and visually appealing templates that reflect your brand's visual identity and are easy to read on any device.

- **Clear calls to action** : Include clear and convincing CTAs (call-to-actions) that direct readers to the next step, whether visiting your website, watching a video or making a purchase.

- **Automation and personalization** : Use automation to send emails at strategic moments, such as welcoming new subscribers or abandoned cart reminders, personalizing messages based on users' actions.

TESTING AND OPTIMIZATION

- **A/B Testing** : Experiment with different subject lines, designs, and content to see what drives the most engagement and conversion.

- **Analysis and tuning** : Monitor performance metrics and use the insights collected to continually refine your email marketing strategy.

INTEGRATING EMAIL WITH OTHER STRATEGIES

For a truly integrated cross-platform content strategy, ensure your email marketing is aligned with your content on social media, blogs, and other digital channels. This not only reinforces your brand message, but also offers multiple touchpoints to engage your audience at different stages of the customer journey.

Equipped with strategies for integrated and effective email marketing, the next step is to explore how to maximize the reach and impact of your content through "**PARTNERSHIPS AND COLLABORATIONS**". In the next chapter, we'll discuss how to leverage relationships with influencers, brands, and platforms to expand your audience and enrich your content with new perspectives.

Get ready to open the doors to new opportunities for growth and innovation, expanding your network and exploring the potential for strategic collaborations in the digital world. Join us on this journey, adding another layer of sophistication to your online communication strategy.

PARTNERSHIPS AND COLLABORATIONS

Exploring strategic partnerships and collaborations can be a powerful way to expand the reach of your content, introduce your brand to new audiences, and enrich your content offering with diverse perspectives. This chapter covers how you can identify, establish, and nurture productive partnerships that complement and amplify your digital content strategy.

THE STRENGTH OF PARTNERSHIPS

- **Access to new audiences** : Collaborating with influencers, complementary brands or platforms can open doors to audiences who might not have discovered your content otherwise.

- **Credibility and trust** : Associating with established and respected names in your industry can elevate your brand's perception and build trust with a wider audience.

- **Enriched content** : Collaborations offer the opportunity to create unique and valuable content by combining expertise and resources.

IDENTIFYING POTENTIAL PARTNERS

- **Values alignment** : Look for partners whose values and mission are in line with those of your brand, ensuring a harmonious and authentic collaboration.

- **Complementarity** : Partners who offer products, services or knowledge complementary to yours can open up opportunities for interesting and valuable collaborative content.

- **Audience engagement** : Consider the level of engagement and relevance of the partner's audience in relation to your own target audience.

ESTABLISHING SUCCESSFUL COLLABORATIONS

- **Clear value proposition** : When approaching potential

partners, present a clear value proposition that highlights the mutual benefits of collaboration.

- **Open and continuous communication** : Effective communication is fundamental to the success of any partnership. Set clear expectations and maintain open lines of communication.

- **Joint planning** : Work together to develop a content plan that leverages the strengths of both parties, ensuring content is relevant and engaging for both audiences.

EXAMPLES OF EFFECTIVE COLLABORATIONS

- **Cross-Campaigns** : Launch a joint promotional or content campaign, sharing it across both platforms to double the reach.

- **Content exchange** : Create content for each other's blog, channel or social network, presenting new perspectives and value to the audience.

- **Joint events or webinars** : Organizing online or physical events in partnership can generate high added value and engagement for the audiences involved.

MEASURING THE SUCCESS OF COLLABORATIONS

Establish clear success metrics before starting the partnership, including increased reach, engagement, audience growth or conversions. Use analytical tools to monitor performance and evaluate the impact of collaboration.

Understanding the power of partnerships and collaborations opens up a new world of possibilities for expanding and enriching your digital content. Next, in the chapter "**VIRTUAL EVENTS AND WEBINARS**", we will explore how you can use online events as an extension of your partnership strategies and as a powerful way to engage and expand your audience.

Get ready to dive into strategies for planning, promoting and executing successful virtual events, using them as a dynamic tool for communication and engagement in the digital universe. Move forward with us on this journey of discovery and continuous innovation.

VIRTUAL EVENTS AND WEBINARS

Virtual events and webinars are exceptional tools for deepening engagement with your audience, educating on relevant topics, and demonstrating expertise. They offer an interactive platform to connect directly with your audience, allowing the exchange of information in real time and strengthening the community around your brand or message. In this chapter, we'll explore how to plan, promote, and deliver virtual events and webinars that capture attention and encourage participation from your audience.

BENEFITS OF VIRTUAL EVENTS AND WEBINARS

- **Global reach** : The online nature of these events removes geographic barriers, allowing people from anywhere in the world to participate.

- **Interactivity** : Tools such as live chats, polls and question and answer (Q&A) sessions enable direct interaction, making the event more engaging and personal.

- **Lead generation** : Virtual events and webinars are excellent for collecting contact information from interested participants, expanding your lead base.

- **Reusable content** : Events can be recorded and used later as on-demand content, multiplying the value of your initial effort.

PLANNING YOUR VIRTUAL EVENT OR WEBINAR

- **Define your goals** : Clarify what you hope to achieve from the event — whether it's educating about a product, discussing industry trends, or building community.

- **Choose the right platform** : Select a webinar or virtual event platform that meets your needs, considering number of participants, interaction tools and customization options.

- **Develop engaging content** : Plan your event content carefully to ensure it is informative, relevant and interactive.

Consider inviting expert speakers or partners to add value.

- **Promotion** : Use your social media channels, email marketing and website to promote the event. Also consider partnerships to expand your reach.

TIPS FOR HOLDING SUCCESSFUL VIRTUAL EVENTS AND WEBINARS

- **Technical test** : Perform technical tests before the event to avoid problems with audio, video or connection.

- **Active engagement** : Encourage audience participation with questions, polls and discussions to make the event more dynamic.

- **Feedback and follow-up** : After the event, solicit feedback from attendees and send follow-up materials such as event recordings, additional resources, and thanks for participating.

MEASURING SUCCESS

Define success metrics specific to your event, such as number of registrants, participation rate, engagement during the event, and post-event feedback. Analyze this data to understand what worked well and what can be improved for future events.

Virtual events and webinars not only enrich your content strategy, but also open doors to new forms of interaction and engagement. In the next chapter, "**AUGMENTED AND VIRTUAL REALITY**", we will explore how these emerging technologies can be used to create even more immersive and memorable experiences for your audience.

Get ready to push the limits of what is possible by using augmented and virtual reality as innovative tools on your digital journey. Move forward with us as we continue to explore the vast territory of effective digital communication.

AUGMENTED AND VIRTUAL REALITY

Augmented reality (AR) and virtual reality (VR) are redefining the boundaries of digital experience, offering new and exciting ways to engage and immerse audiences. These technologies allow you to create unique experiences that can enrich your content strategy, highlight your brand and provide significant value to your users. In this chapter, we'll explore how you can incorporate augmented and virtual reality into your digital communication to create memorable and interactive experiences.

UNDERSTANDING AR AND VR

- **Augmented reality (AR)** : Superimposes digital information on the real world, enriching the user's reality with virtual elements. Examples include social media filters and apps that let you view products in a real space.

- **Virtual reality (VR)** : Creates a fully immersive environment, usually accessed through a VR headset, where users can interact with a completely digital world.

BENEFITS OF INCORPORATION OF AR AND VR

- **Immersive experiences** : AR and VR offer unique ways to tell stories and present information, creating deeply immersive experiences.

- **Competitive differentiation** : Using these technologies can differentiate your brand, showcasing innovation and improving customer engagement.

- **Improved education and training** : VR, in particular, offers exceptional opportunities for training and education, allowing for realistic, hands-on simulations.

- **Viral potential** : Unique AR and VR experiences have high potential for social sharing, increasing the organic reach of your content.

IMPLEMENTING AR AND VR INTO CONTENT STRATEGY

- **Start small** : Experiment with AR filters on social media or simple virtual tours to understand how your audience interacts with these technologies.

- **Focus on value for the user** : AR and VR experiences should enrich existing content, offering clear additional value for the user.

- **Strategic Partnerships** : Collaborate with AR/VR developers and creators to explore creative and technically viable ideas that complement your brand and content goals.

- **Promote your experiences** : Utilize all of your communication channels to promote your AR and VR initiatives, encouraging user testing and feedback.

CHALLENGES AND CONSIDERATIONS

- **Accessibility** : Consider the accessibility of your AR and VR experiences, both in terms of hardware requirements and ease of use.

- **Investment** : Evaluate cost versus benefit, as developing AR and VR experiences can require significant investment.

- **Measurement of success** : Define clear metrics to evaluate the success of your initiatives, such as engagement, conversions or increase in interaction time.

By incorporating augmented and virtual reality into your content strategy, you open up new dimensions of interactivity and engagement. In the next chapter, **"COMMUNITY MANAGEMENT**," we'll discuss how to manage and cultivate an engaged community, a crucial aspect of maximizing the impact of your content and emerging technologies like AR and VR.

Be prepared to learn best practices in building and maintaining a vibrant community, as effective communication and an engaged audience are critical to success in the dynamic digital world.

Continue with us on this journey of innovation and discovery.

COMMUNITY MANAGEMENT

Cultivating an engaged community isn't just about building numbers; it's about fostering meaningful relationships with your audience, creating a space for dialogue, support and sharing ideas. A strong community can become the foundation for the lasting success of your brand or message. In this chapter, we'll explore effective strategies for community management that will help strengthen those bonds and maintain engagement.

THE IMPORTANCE OF COMMUNITY MANAGEMENT

- **Deep engagement** : A well-managed community promotes a level of engagement that goes beyond passive content consumption, encouraging active interaction between members and with the brand.

- **Valuable feedback** : Communities provide direct insights into your audience's needs, wants, and perceptions, serving as a vital channel for feedback.

- **Brand Advocacy** : Happy and engaged community members can become advocates for your brand by sharing your content and recommending your products or services.

STRATEGIES FOR EFFECTIVE COMMUNITY MANAGEMENT

- **Establish clear norms** : Define and communicate community rules to ensure a respectful and welcoming environment where everyone feels safe to participate.

- **Foster interactivity** : Encourage discussions, ask questions, and create opportunities for members to interact with each other and the brand. This may include Q&A sessions, challenges and virtual events.

- **Recognize and reward** : Show appreciation for community participation by recognizing significant contributions and, when possible, rewarding activity that benefits the group.

- **Active moderation** : Monitor the community to quickly respond to questions, resolve conflicts, and ensure interactions remain positive and constructive.

- **Exclusive content** : Offer additional value to your community with access to exclusive content, previews or special opportunities, strengthening the sense of belonging.

- **Use community management tools** : Digital tools can help manage the community more efficiently, facilitating communication, content scheduling and engagement analysis.

BUILDING AND MAINTAINING CONNECTIONS

- **Actively listen** : Keep an eye on conversations within your community. Member feedback is crucial for adapting strategies and content to audience needs.

- **Be authentic** : Authentic and transparent communication helps build trust and loyalty. Be honest about challenges and open in your communications.

- **Sustainable growth** : Focus on organic and sustainable growth of the community, prioritizing the quality of interactions over quantity.

Effective community management is an essential component of any successful content strategy, creating a solid foundation of support, engagement and loyalty. As we move into "**CONTENT ACCESSIBILITY**", the next chapter will focus on how to ensure your content is inclusive and accessible to all, respecting diversity and promoting equal access to information.

Get ready to explore best practices and tools that can make your digital content accessible to broader audiences, including people with disabilities. Continue with us on this inclusive journey, learning how to expand the impact and reach of your content in the digital universe.

CONTENT ACCESSIBILITY

Accessibility in the digital context goes beyond social responsibility; it is an opportunity to reach and engage a wider audience, including people with disabilities. Making your content accessible means more people can benefit from, learn from, and interact with your brand or message. In this chapter, we'll explore how to ensure your digital content is inclusive and accessible to everyone.

UNDERSTANDING ACCESSIBILITY

Accessibility refers to the creation of digital content and platforms that can be easily used by people with a wide range of abilities, including those with visual, hearing, motor or cognitive disabilities. This involves considering multiple aspects of design and content, ensuring everyone can navigate, understand and interact with your content without barriers.

PRINCIPLES OF ACCESSIBILITY

- **Perceivable** : Ensure information is presented in a way that everyone can understand, including using alternative text for images and captions for videos.

- **Operable** : Ensure that the interface can be operated by any user, which may include keyboard navigation and sufficient time to read and use the content.

- **Understandable** : Make the content easy to understand by using clear, predictable language and explaining any jargon or abbreviations.

- **Robust** : Develop content that can be reliably interpreted by a wide range of users, including those who rely on assistive technologies.

STRATEGIES TO MAKE CONTENT ACCESSIBLE

- **Use alternative texts** : Provide clear and concise descriptions for images, graphics and other visual content, allowing people with visual impairments to understand their context.

- Transcriptions and subtitles : Offer transcriptions for audio content and subtitles for videos, ensuring that people with hearing impairments can access the information.

- Text Contrast and Size : Ensure adequate contrast between text and background and allow text size to be adjusted for easier reading.

- Simplified navigation : Structure your content logically and provide multiple forms of navigation, such as menus, search and sitemap.

- Testing and feedback : Carry out regular accessibility tests, preferably with the participation of people with disabilities, and be open to feedback to continually improve.

TOOLS AND RESOURCES

Several tools and guidelines are available to help make your content accessible, including Web Content Accessibility Guidelines (WCAG) and accessibility testing software that can automate the identification of common issues.

By making digital content more accessible, you not only expand your reach, but also demonstrate a commitment to inclusion and equality. Moving forward to "**SUSTAINABILITY AND SOCIAL RESPONSIBILITY**," we'll explore how to incorporate these important values into your content strategy, strengthening your connection with your audience and highlighting your brand as socially responsible.

Continue on this journey with us as we delve deeper into how digital content can be a force for good, promoting sustainable and responsible practices that resonate with your audience's contemporary concerns.

SUSTAINABILITY AND SOCIAL RESPONSIBILITY

Incorporating sustainability and social responsibility into your content strategy is not just a way to contribute to a better world; it also strengthens the connection with its audience, who are increasingly aware and concerned about environmental and social issues. This chapter will discuss how you can use your digital content to reflect and promote sustainable and responsible practices, positioning your brand as an agent of positive change.

THE IMPORTANCE OF SUSTAINABILITY AND SOCIAL RESPONSIBILITY

- **Authentic connection with the public** : Consumers and users value brands that demonstrate genuine concern for the environment and the community. Communicating your sustainability and social responsibility initiatives can strengthen this connection.

- **Differentiation in the market** : By positioning yourself as a responsible brand, you can stand out in a competitive market, attracting consumers who make choices based on values.

- **Positive impact** : In addition to the benefits for the brand, promoting sustainability and social responsibility contributes to a positive impact on the world, encouraging others to adopt more conscious practices.

INCORPORATING SUSTAINABILITY AND SOCIAL RESPONSIBILITY INTO CONTENT

- **Communicate your practices** : Be transparent about the actions your brand is taking to be more sustainable and socially responsible. This can include everything from environmentally friendly operations to supporting social causes.

- **Educate your audience** : Use your content to educate about the importance of sustainability and social responsibility. This could involve sharing practical tips, information about environmental and social issues, or stories of positive impact.

- **Promote positive actions** : Encourage your audience to adopt sustainable practices in their own lives. This can be done through challenges, fundraising initiatives, or awareness campaigns.

- **Partnerships with aligned organizations** : Collaborate with NGOs, nonprofits, or other businesses that share similar values to amplify your impact and reach.

- **Show impact** : Regularly report on the progress of your initiatives, showing the tangible impact of your actions. This may include case studies, sustainability reports and success stories.

CHALLENGES AND CONSIDERATIONS

- **Authenticity** : Make sure your sustainability and social responsibility initiatives are genuine and reflect your brand's values to avoid accusations of "greenwashing" or social exploitation.

- **Continuous engagement** : The commitment to sustainability and social responsibility must be continuous, not just a one-off campaign. Integrate these values deeply into your brand and content strategy.

- **Accessibility** : Consider how to make your initiatives inclusive and accessible to a broad audience, ensuring everyone can participate and contribute.

By embracing sustainability and social responsibility in your content strategy, you not only strengthen your brand, but also contribute to building a better future. The next chapter, "**CRISIS MANAGEMENT**," will cover how to effectively prepare for and respond to potential crises related to your content or brand, ensuring you maintain your audience's trust and support, even in challenging times.

Step forward with us as we explore crisis management in the digital context, equipping you with strategies to navigate difficult situations with grace and resilience.

CRISIS MANAGEMENT

No business or brand is immune to crises, but the way you prepare and respond can make all the difference in preserving your audience's trust and loyalty. Effective crisis management is essential to minimizing potential damage to your reputation and operations. This chapter provides strategies for managing crises related to your digital content or brand, ensuring clear and effective communication during challenging times.

UNDERSTANDING CRISIS MANAGEMENT

Crisis management involves identifying potential threats to your brand, preparing advance action plans, and communicating effectively with your audience and stakeholders during a crisis. Rapid preparation and response can help mitigate negative impact and even turn a crisis into an opportunity to strengthen your brand perception.

CRISIS PREPAREDNESS STRATEGIES

- **Crisis management plan** : Develop a comprehensive plan that includes potential scenarios, response protocols, clear lines of communication, and a dedicated crisis management team.

- **Monitoring and early warning** : Use digital monitoring tools to keep an eye on mentions of your brand, allowing for early detection of potential crises.

- **Internal communication** : Make sure your team is well informed about crisis management plans and knows how to act and who to communicate in the event of an emergency.

RESPONDING TO CRISES

- **Quick response** : A timely response is crucial. Acknowledge the situation quickly, even if it's just to let them know you're aware of the problem and more information will follow.

- **Transparency and honesty** : Be transparent about the nature of the crisis, what is being done to resolve it and what will be done to avoid similar situations in the future.

- **Coherent communication** : Maintain a consistent message across all communication channels, whether social media, email or press statements.

- **Focus on the audience** : Understand your audience's concerns and questions and address them directly in your communication.

- **Post-crisis assessment** : After the crisis, evaluate the performance of your response, identify lessons learned, and adjust your crisis management plan as needed.

PRACTICAL CASES

- **Online reputation management** : Monitor and respond to negative reviews on social media in a professional and constructive manner, showing commitment to improvement.

- **Product recalls** : In the event of a recall, proactively communicate with affected consumers, offering clear solutions and compensation where appropriate.

Navigating a crisis requires preparation, transparency and effective communication. With these strategies in hand, you are better equipped to manage difficult situations while maintaining your audience's trust. In the next chapter, "**FUTURE TRENDS IN DIGITAL CONTENT**," we'll look to the horizon, exploring how to stay ahead in an ever-evolving digital world, anticipating trends and future-proofing your content strategy.

Be ready to embark on a journey into the future of digital content, where innovation and continuous adaptation will be your greatest tools for continued success and growth. Stay with us as we explore what the future holds for the digital world.

FUTURE TRENDS IN DIGITAL CONTENT

As the digital world continues to evolve rapidly, staying up to date with the latest trends is crucial to ensuring your content strategy remains relevant and effective. This chapter explores emerging trends in digital content and offers insights into how to prepare for future changes, ensuring your brand or message continues to resonate with your audience.

ARTIFICIAL INTELLIGENCE AND MACHINE LEARNING

AI and machine learning are transforming the way we create and personalize content. These technologies allow the analysis of large volumes of data to better understand audience preferences, optimize content delivery and even generate automated content that adapts to users' needs.

AUGMENTED AND VIRTUAL REALITY

As previously discussed, AR and VR are creating new opportunities for immersive content experiences. As these technologies become more accessible, expect to see an increase in their use to tell stories, educate and promote products in innovative ways.

INTERACTIVE CONTENT

Content that allows direct user interaction is becoming increasingly popular. Tools like quizzes, polls, interactive calculators and games can increase engagement while providing valuable insights into your audience's preferences and behaviors.

SHORT-TERM VIDEO AND VERTICAL FORMATS

Influenced by the success of platforms like TikTok and Instagram Stories, short-form video and vertical formats are solidifying as key preferences among content consumers, especially among the younger generation.

SUSTAINABILITY AND SOCIAL RESPONSIBILITY

As discussed previously, sustainability and social responsibility will continue to be important topics. Content that demonstrates your brand's commitment to these issues can strengthen connections with audiences who value ethics and environmental action.

CUSTOMIZATION AT SCALE

Expectation for personalized content experiences is growing. Using data and technology to create content that meets each user's individual interests, without sacrificing scale, will be a key trend.

DATA PRIVACY AND TRANSPARENCY

As awareness about data privacy increases, brands will need to be transparent about how they collect, use and protect user information, balancing personalization with privacy.

PREPARING FOR THE FUTURE

- **Keep learning** : Stay informed about the latest trends and technologies through continuous education and experimentation.

- **Flexibility and adaptation** : Be ready to adapt your strategy as the digital landscape evolves, experimenting with new ideas and formats.

- **Listen to your audience** : Use feedback and data analysis to understand your audience's changing preferences and adjust your content accordingly.

As we explore future trends in digital content, it's crucial to look ahead with a mindset of innovation and adaptation. In the next and final chapter, "**CONTENT MONETIZATION**", we will cover strategies for transforming your digital content into a viable source of revenue, ensuring the long-term sustainability of your content initiatives.

Be ready to discover how to maximize the return on your

investment in digital content, balancing creativity, engagement and economic viability. Step forward with us as we complete our journey through the facets of digital content strategy.

CONTENT MONETIZATION

As we develop and implement digital content strategies, a crucial consideration is how this content can not only engage and grow our audience, but also contribute to the financial sustainability of our initiatives. In this final chapter, we'll explore several content monetization strategies, offering insights into how to turn your content into a viable source of revenue.

CONTENT MONETIZATION STRATEGIES

- **Advertising and sponsorships** : Integrating paid advertising into your content or obtaining sponsorships from related brands are direct forms of monetization. The key is to maintain content relevance and integrity by choosing partners that add value to your audience.

- **Subscriptions and premium content** : Offering a paid subscription for access to exclusive or premium content can generate recurring revenue, especially if you've already established a high perceived value in your free content.

– **Selling products or services** : Use your content as a platform to promote and sell related products or services. This can include everything from branded merchandise to online courses and consultancies.

- **Affiliates** : Earn commissions by promoting third-party products or services that are relevant to your audience. Transparency is crucial, so be sure to disclose affiliate relationships.

- **Crowdfunding and direct support** : Platforms like Patreon allow creators to receive direct financial support from their audience, in exchange for access to exclusive content and other rewards.

- **Content Licensing** : If you create original, high-quality content, another company may be interested in licensing it for their own uses, generating an additional source of revenue.

CONSIDERATIONS FOR EFFECTIVE MONETIZATION

- **Value for the audience** : Regardless of the monetization strategy chosen, it is essential that it offers additional value to your audience and does not compromise the quality or integrity of your content.

- **Diversification** : Don't depend on a single source of income. Diversifying your monetization strategies can help minimize risk and maximize revenue potential.

- **Transparency** : Be transparent with your audience about how your content is monetized. Trust is a crucial component of the relationship with the public.

- **Adaptation and experimentation** : Be prepared to experiment and adapt your monetization strategies based on audience feedback and financial performance.

With the right strategies, digital content is not only a powerful tool for engaging and growing your audience, but also a viable source of revenue. As we complete our journey through the many facets of digital content strategy, we hope that you are now equipped with the knowledge and tools necessary to not only create meaningful content, but also sustain your initiatives financially.

We remember that success in monetizing digital content, as with all aspects of content strategy, requires passion, perseverance and a willingness to continually learn and adapt. Move forward with confidence, knowing that every piece of content you create contributes not only to the growth of your brand or message, but also to a deeper connection with those your work aims to serve.

Be ready to navigate the future of digital content, embracing the opportunities and challenges ahead. Thank you for joining us on this journey of exploration and discovery into the art and science of digital content.

FINAL CONSIDERATIONS

We completed the detailed journey through the universe of digital content strategy, covering everything from content production and distribution to monetization techniques. This path is designed to equip you with a comprehensive understanding of how to create, promote and monetize content in an ever-changing digital environment.

Now, looking ahead, we encourage you to continue exploring, learning and adapting. The digital world never stops evolving, and staying up to date with the latest trends, technologies and practices is crucial to continued success.

CONTINUING THE JOURNEY

- **Stay informed** : Stay aware of the latest trends in digital technology, content marketing and consumer behavior. Trusted sources and thought leaders in the industry can be invaluable resources.

- **Experiment** : Don't be afraid to test new ideas, formats or platforms. Experimentation is key to discovering what resonates with your audience.

- **Listen to your audience** : Use feedback and engagement data to continually adjust and refine your strategy. A user-centric approach will always prevail.

- **Continuing education** : Consider courses, webinars, and other learning opportunities to advance your skills and knowledge in specific areas of interest.

- **Collaboration** : Stay open to partnerships and collaborations that can enrich your content and expand your reach.

We hope this journey has been informative and inspiring, providing you with the tools and knowledge you need to confidently move forward with your own digital content strategies. Remember, the path to success is continuous and always evolving. With passion, creativity, and dedication, you can build a strong, meaningful digital presence that not only reaches, but truly engages and inspires your audience.

Thank you for joining us on this comprehensive exploration of digital content strategy. We're excited to see where your journey takes you and how you'll use what you learn to create, share, and thrive in the digital world. Keep exploring, creating and innovating – the future of digital content is bright and waiting for you.

FINAL CONSIDERATIONS AND FUTURE STEPS

As you move forward, here are some guidelines to keep your content relevant and your marketing strategy effective:

- **Continuous innovation** : The digital world is constantly changing, with new technologies and platforms emerging regularly. Stay innovative by experimenting with new ideas and adapting to change.

- **Feedback and iteration** : Use your audience's feedback to continually improve your content. Iterating based on detailed analysis and audience responses can help you refine your approach and better meet your audience's needs.

- **Education and professional development** : Commit to ongoing education in the area of digital marketing and content creation. Webinars, online courses, conferences, and up-to-date reading are excellent ways to keep your skills sharp and your strategy up to date.

- **Network and community** : Building and maintaining a network of professionals in the field can provide valuable insights, collaboration opportunities and support. Actively participate in online communities, discussion groups and industry events.

- **Sustainability and responsibility** : As your content

strategy evolves, continue to emphasize the importance of sustainability and social responsibility in your communication. This not only reinforces your brand's reputation, but also contributes positively to society and the environment.

This manual was created to serve as a guide through the complex and dynamic world of digital content marketing. Thank you for joining us on this learning journey. We hope the strategies, ideas, and best practices discussed here inspire you to create impactful content, build meaningful relationships with your audience, and successfully achieve your marketing goals.

The future of digital content is bright and full of possibilities. With the right tools, a strategic approach and a dose of creativity, you are well positioned to be part of this exciting future. Move forward with confidence, exploring new ideas, embracing change, and creating content that resonates, educates, and inspires. The next chapter in your content marketing journey begins now, and you will write it.

As we turn the final page of this journey together, I sincerely hope that the learnings shared here have touched your heart and sparked new perspectives. If this book has brought you any value, I kindly ask that you take a few moments to leave a review on Amazon. Your words not only help me grow and hone my craft, but they also guide other readers in their quests for knowledge and inspiration. Your opinion is a valuable gift, both for me and for the community of readers looking for stories that transform. I sincerely thank you for sharing this journey with me and I hope we can meet again in the pages of a new adventure.

REGINALDO OSNILDO

Hello, I'm Reginaldo Osnildo, author and innovator in the fields of sales, technology, and communication strategies. My background spans from the academic setting, as a professor and researcher at the University of Southern Santa Catarina, to hands-on strategy development at the Catarinense Radio Group. With a PhD in sales narratives and digital convergence, and a Master's in storytelling and social imaginary, I offer my readers a unique blend of theory and practice. My aim is to deliver knowledge in a simple, practical, and didactic language, encouraging direct application in one's personal and professional life.

Yours sincerely

Reginaldo Osnildo

+55 48 991913865

reginaldoosnildo@gmail.com

www.ingramcontent.com/pod-product-compliance
Lightning Source LLC
Chambersburg PA
CBHW050327230526
45471CB00005B/2380